WILDFIRES

A TRUE BOOK

by
**Paul P. and
Diane M. Sipiera**

Children's Press®

A Division of Grolier Publishing

New York London Hong Kong Sydney
Danbury, Connecticut

Firefighters leave
a smoky forest

Reading Consultant
Linda Cornwell
*Learning Resource Consultant
Indiana Department
of Education*

Authors' Dedication
*To our little wildfire,
Paula Frances Sipiera*

Visit Children's Press® on the Internet at:
http://publishing.grolier.com

Library of Congress Cataloging-in-Publication Data

Sipiera, Paul P.
    Wildfires / by Paul P. and Diane M. Sipiera.
        p.   cm.   —   (A true book)
    Includes bibliographical references and index.
    Summary: Discusses the conditions which cause wildfires, ways to con-
trol them, and their damaging as well as beneficial effects. Includes a
chapter on the forest fire in Yellowstone National Park in 1988.
    ISBN: 0-516-20682-6 (lib. bdg.)   0-516-26445-1 (pbk.)
    1. Wildfires—Juvenile literature.   [1. Wildfires. 2. Forest fires.
3. Fires.]   I. Sipiera, Diane M.   II. Title.   III. Series.
SD421.23.S57   1998
577.2—dc21   97-37150
                                                                              CIP
                                                                              AC

Contents

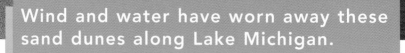

Wind and water have worn away these sand dunes along Lake Michigan.

Powers of Nature

Nature works each day in many ways that affect Earth. Some of nature's actions happen slowly. Most people do not notice they are taking place. These actions include the work of wind and water as they erode (wear away) the landscape.

Other changes on Earth happen more quickly. An earthquake can destroy a city or cause a giant landslide. A volcano can explode with great force, and cause terrible destruction. Even violent storms such as hurricanes and tornadoes can cause severe damage to a town or a city.

Another change Earth experiences happens through wildfires. There are two kinds of wildfires: forest fires and

This landslide, which occurred in Wyoming in 1997, flowed across the highway for several days.

A forest fire in Florida (top), and a brush fire in California (bottom)

brush fires. Forest fires occur in areas of land where there are tall trees and vast wilderness. Brush fires occur in areas of land where small trees and shrubs grow. When a forest fire breaks out, it can destroy thousands of acres of land. The wildlife of the area is also threatened. A brush fire that gets out of control can spread into areas where people live, and destroy their homes.

Causes of Wildfires

A wildfire can begin in many ways. Most often, it is the result of a lightning strike. However, many wildfires are started by careless people. Sometimes people do not put their campfires out completely. This can cause nearby shrubs or trees to catch fire.

This forest fire burned more than 10,000 acres (4,000 hectares) of Colorado's Pike National Forest. The fire was caused by human activity.

Wildfires can also be caused by people who throw away lit cigarettes. These cigarettes can burn grass or bushes. If

Campers in wooded areas must be considerate of their surroundings.

the fires burn out of control, huge wildfires can result. Campers, hikers, and picnickers must be careful to keep accidental fires from starting.

Sometimes people set fires on purpose. Farmers light fires on their land to burn off weeds and dead wood. Farmers usually watch these fires carefully. They keep plenty of water nearby to put the fires out.

This fire, set to clear an area of prairie, is called a controlled burn.

Some people set fires to destroy homes or property. This is against the law. When these people are caught, they may be severely punished.

Wildfires can be started naturally by lightning strikes. When lightning strikes a tree, the tree can be set on fire. The same is true for dry prairie grass. Sometimes lightning hits the ground, and sets the grass on fire. Wind makes the flames spread. A

This tree was struck by lightning. (The path of the lightning bolt is visible on the trunk.)

prairie, or brush, fire can rage over a large area.

The weather in a certain place also plays a part in the occurrence of wildfires. Whether an area is usually dry

When prairie grass (above) or brush gets extremely dry, it is more likely to catch fire. Pine trees explode into flames as a result of the burning resin (right).

or wet is important. Fires start easily in places where there is a long dry season without much rain. Natural fires do not start easily in tropical areas because there is a lot of rain.

Another important factor is the kind of trees that grow in an area. Pine trees burn more easily than other trees. This is because pine trees contain a substance called resin (REZ-in). Resin is very flammable. This means it is likely to catch fire. When a wildfire burns through a pine forest, the high temperature burns the resin. The trees then explode into flames.

Dangers from Wildfires

As wildfires spread over large areas, homes and other buildings may be destroyed. This can cause millions of dollars worth of damage to land and property.

Fighting wildfires is dangerous and expensive. There is always the danger that firefighters and others may be killed.

An approaching wildfire threatens buildings of the University of California in Irvine (top). One firefighter (left) attempts to control the wildfire that threatens a fire engine, as well as the firefighter inside.

A large white home sits undamaged surrounded by homes that burned to the ground during devastating wildfires in southern California in 1993. The owner of the house stood on the roof, and used a garden hose to put out approaching flames.

In the United States, wildfires commonly occur during dry seasons. The fires spread quickly through the brush. High winds also make the fires spread.

Bush Fires

Much of Australia is dry, brush-covered land. There, wildfires are called bush fires. When a fire begins, it can burn millions of acres of brush. Often, there is little people can do to put the fire out. Animals such as kangaroos and emus flee from the flames. Any sheep or cattle stations, or ranches, in the path of the fire will be lost. If the fire gets close to a city, people may fear for their lives and their homes.

A firefighter watches a bush fire burn near Sydney, Australia.

Anything in the path of the flames will be destroyed, including homes. It is hard for people to protect their homes because during the dry season there may not be enough water to fight the fire.

Smaller wildfires can burn along roads and highways. People in passing automobiles sometimes throw lit cigarettes out into the brush along the road. A brush fire can start, and quickly burn its way along the road. The smoke from the fire may cover the road. This makes driving difficult as cars pass through the smoke.

Firefighters battle a brush fire along a California road.

Controlling Wildfires

Once a wildfire breaks out, firefighters are quickly called into action. One of the first things they do is cut a fire break. Firefighters cut down and clear all the brush and trees along a line in front of the fire. They hope that once the fire reaches the break, it

A firefighter uses a chain saw to clear a fire break.

will have nothing to burn. Unless wind blows the fire across the fire break, it will slowly burn out.

Another way to fight a wildfire is to set a backfire. Firefighters use tools called drip-torches to light a small fire in the path of a large fire. The backfire burns toward the approaching wildfire. It burns the trees and brush in the wildfire's path. As a result, the wildfire has no fuel to

Backfires are set
with a tool called
a drip-torch.

These firefighters are using a hose to spray water on a fire.

continue burning. Firefighters can then work to control the fire, and to put it out.

At the fire, firefighters will either throw soil or use water to put out the flames.

Airplanes may also be used to dump large amounts of water on the fire. Some airplanes dump a special chemical that puts out fires. One group of brave firefighters is called the

A plane dumps a special chemical on a forest fire in an attempt to put it out.

"smoke jumpers." They parachute close to the fire from low-flying airplanes. Their quick action to put out the fire can keep it from burning out of control.

One way to control wildfires is to keep them from starting. In many places where wildfires are common, a fire-hazard warning is posted. A color code is often used to show people what the fire danger is on a particular day.

Red means that the danger is high. It is a reminder to campers and others to be extra careful with their use of fire. Green means that the fire danger is low. A fire is not likely to start.

One of the worst wildfires in U.S. history occurred during the summer of 1988 at Yellowstone National Park, Wyoming. For months, the weather there had been hot and dry. As a result, lightning started more than forty-five fires. Other fires were started

Yellowstone, established in 1872, was the world's first national park.

The fires at Yellowstone burned more than 1 million acres (567,000 hectares) of land.

y careless people. Strong winds spread the fires. ames seemed to leap from place to place. Soon, ellowstone was swallowed up by a huge forest e. Pine forests that had grown for hundreds of ears were destroyed in minutes.

Firefighters from all over the United States worked day and night to control the fire. But they couldn't put it out completely. Finally, in September, the moist, fall weather set in. Light snow fell. Nature helped to end the great fire.

Part of the burned area after the fires ended

Damage to Land and Wildlife

A wildfire such as the one that occurred at Yellowstone National-al Park can have a serious effect on the environment. In only one day, the Yellowstone fire burned more land than all of the fires that had occurred there in the last one hundred years. The

Smoke from a wildfire fills the sky.

damage mostly affected the wildlife. As the fire raged, most large animals sensed the danger. They fled from the flames. Animals that burrow

Many animals, such as these elk, couldn't find enough food in the burned-out forest.

into the ground also remained safe. The big problem occurred after the fire. By destroying the forest and plant life, the animals' food was lost. Without enough food, many animals died from starvation. When spring arrived, new plants grew and provided food.

New plant growth after a fire brings food to forest animals.

A wildfire rages close to a house, which was later burned to the ground. (The family living here escaped unharmed.)

Wildfires do more than just destroy buildings and property. Damage from wildfires includes the death of wildlife. Trees are lost. Land is ruined. People's outdoor activities, such as hik-ing or camping, are interrupted.

What Is Good About Wildfires?

There are ways that wildfires can be good for the land. A forest may need fire to keep it alive. In a forest, fallen leaves, branches, and trees begin to build up. This build-up provides shelter and food for insects, bacteria, and tree

seedlings. When a fire occurs, the build-up burns away. The fire "cleans" the forest. As a result, there is more room for plants and trees to grow.

Some pine trees need fire to open their seed cones. As

the cones fall to the ground, they are tightly closed. The heat of a forest fire makes the cones pop open. The seeds fall out, and new trees can grow.

A new pine tree grows next to the burned trunks of pine trees that were destroyed by fire.

Fire can also help to spread seeds over prairies or grass-lands. Fires destroy unwanted plants. New plants, such as wildflowers and prairie grasses, can grow.

New grass and wildflowers grow in a burned area of forest.

Hopefully, this young pine tree will not be destroyed by a wildfire before it has a chance to grow to its full size.

Fire can be both good and bad for forests and grasslands. It is important that all of the land is protected from careless people and accidental fires.

To Find Out More

Here are some additional resources to help you learn more about wildfires:

Books

Davis, Kay and Wendy Oldsfield. **Weather.** Raintree Steck-Vaughn, 1991.

Fraser, Mary. **Forest Fire!** Fulcrum Publishing, 1996.

Greene, Carol. **Firefighters.** Child's World, 1996.

Kramer, Stephen. **Lightning.** Lerner, 1993.

Petersen, David. **Yellowstone National Park.** Children's Press, 1992.

Simon, Seymour. **Wildfires.** Morrow Junior Books, 1996.

Organizations and Online Sites

USDA Forest Service
United States Department
of Agriculture
14th and Independence
Avenue, SW
Washington, DC   20250
http://www.fs.fed.us

National Park Service
P. O. Box 37127
Washington, DC   20013
http://www.nps.gov

Yellowstone National Park
P. O. Box 168
Yellowstone National Park,
WY   82190
http://www.nps.gov/yell//

Smokey Bear Forest Fire Prevention
http://www.smokeybear. com

This site offers games and puzzles about campfire safety and forest fire prevention.

Important Words

environment the natural world of the land, sea, and air

hazard a danger or a risk

landscape features such as hills, rivers, valleys, and mountains that make up Earth's surface

lightning bolt of electricity that can occur during a thunderstorm

nature everything in the world that is not made by people, such as plants, animals, and the weather

source place where something comes from

Index

Meet the Authors

Paul and Diane Sipiera share the same interest in science and nature. Paul is a college professor in Palatine, Illinois. Diane is the director of education for the Planetary Studies Foundation of Algonquin, Illinois. Together with their daughters Andrea, Paula, and Carrie Ann, the Sipieras enjoy their small farm in Galena, Illinois.